ORNITHOLOGY

poems by

M. G. Stephens

Finishing Line Press
Georgetown, Kentucky

ORNITHOLOGY

ACKNOWLEDGMENTS

A few of these poems appeared in the magazine Subterranean Blue (Canada)

Publisher: Leah Huete de Maines
Editor: Christen Kincaid
Cover Art: Jobi Petersen Cates
Author Photo: S. E. Wolan
Cover Design: Elizabeth Maines McCleavy

Order online: www.finishinglinepress.com
              also available on amazon.com

Author inquiries and mail orders:
Finishing Line Press
PO Box 1626
Georgetown, Kentucky 40324
USA

Table of Contents

For
Sage
&
Etta

To Bee
(Or not)
To Bee

GOLDFINCHES

Blue skies
Sun out

Goldfinches
Among milkweed

Eight of them
Eight

Such a lucky
Number

THE MESSAGE

If love calls
Should I answer

Or let the machine
Take a message

TRULY

Love is
Absence

Of

Conse-
Quences

Absent

Motives
Minus

Psycho-
Logic-

Al
Is all

Sensa-
Tions

In

The night
Dreams

About you
You

Who knows
Who

I mean
I am

Yours

SMILE

Love smiles
And I

Smile back

Love lies
Down

Next to me
In the heat

Feigns head-
Ache

Talks about
The

South of
France

Nice where
Matisse

Painted

His odalisques
Or

His domestic
Portraits

Such as

Interior at
Nice

MOON

Summer's register
Moon up

Above

Everyone's
In

Love

But is love
Lying or

Just resting

Is love a series
Of faces

De Kooning
Comes

To mind

PURPLE HAZE

Is love
Love

Or is
It

Like

Jimi Hendrix
Said

An illusion

THAT

Is love
Simply

That

ORNITHOLOGY

Gentle birds
In

Trees

Help me
Please

What think
You

On this
This

Theme

Sunrise
Sunset

What happens
Next

Hieronymus
Bosch

Patron saint of
What

Inspiration for
Apocalypse

Grant us
Mercy

Give us
Peace

DELTA

Between
Is that

Which

I want
Think

I need
But

Do I

Do I

Do I really
Need

This delta
Of

Desire

This delta
Of

Love

THE RAIN

I love this
Way and that

Like the rain
Constant

One minute
The next

Not
My love is

Like a
Hammer

Pounding
Pounding

In the
Skull

Love is like
A hammer

Looking
Looking

For a nail
A tale

A turn
This

Sojourn
To

The heart

Break it

Break
It

Open

THE LAMPS

Love is
Out

Beyond the
Lamps

Even among
The tramps

Love blossoms
Burgeoning

In footsteps
Along

The lakefront

SOME TREES

Beyond the trees
Oaks

And maples and ash
And

Acorns fall
Upon

Heads

And he slips
On his

Ass

But love
Makes

It resonate
Percolate

Percuss

Robin's egg
Blue

As sky

In the
Branch

Tiny mouths
To

Feed mother
Robin

HOPE

1.
The opposite
Of love

Is

Not just
Fear

But also
Hope

That
Is

Hopeless

Love is
The

Only thing
To

Pull us
Out

Of

The mire
Before

We perspire
Expire

In the mud
Yet

No one
Said

Love was
Pretty

2.
Sometimes
It

Is as ugly
As rain

After sunshine
Rain

Full of
Acid

Turning

Evergreens
Yellow

3.
This hope
Chest

Is full

Of
Love

Open it
Now

Pan-
Dor-

A

HOPELESS

The world
Is

Not

Just but
I

Still

Live life
My

Life

With hope
And

Hope

And

Even with
More

Hope-
Less-

Ness

And even more
Hope

Hum-
Ming-

Bird

In inner
Court-

Yard this
Morning

THE MACHINE

Do I let the
Machine

Take the call
Is this

The answer

Is love the
Answer

To that question
That

Quest

You did not know
You were

On

MICHAELMAS

In October
After

Michael-
Mas

The morning
Air

Astounds
Ex-

Panding
Lungs

As if
She

Were a
Was like

A teen-
Ager

Which she
Was

Once once
Up-

On a
Time

LISTS

I love
A

List
Of

Any-
Thing

Broc-
Coli

Banan-
As

Gin-
Ger

Apples
And

And
Pears

Your
Ankles

Your
Calves

Your
Back

Neck
Nose

Eyes
Hair

Where
Are

You now
As

I sketch
This

Portrait
Of

What love
Is

A list
Of

Par-
Ticulars

A list
Of

Perfections
Or

Barring
That

Im-
Per-

Fections
So

Perfect-
Ly

A-
Chieved

SMELL

I lost
My

Sense
Of

Smell
Only

I can
Still

Imag-
Ine

Your smell
Even

If it
Is

An imag-
Inary

Sense
Fed

By mem-
Ory

Or twists
Of

The mind
Which

I don't
Mind

The remem-
Brance

So strong
It

Is as
If

I
Smell

Once more
Sweat

Of sex
Red

Under-
Wear

On the
Floor

Next to
The

Bed in
Which

You lay
Naked

SCREECH

A per-

E-
Grine

Fal-
Con

Goes
At

An-
Other

Bird
This

One
A

Sparrow
Pinned

Under
Razor-

Like
Talons

The fal-
Con's

Tal-
Ent

It cuts
Thru

Air at
200

Mph
Like

A bull-
Et

Like a
Knife

Thru but-
Ter

Speed of
Life

Like the
Light

A blur of
Blood

And feath-
ers

POETICS

Poetry
Changes

Nothing

Or put
An-

Other

Way
It

Changes

Every-
Thing

BE STILL

If love calls
Answer

Be
Still

Be open
Close

Your eyes
Imagine

THE GIFT

The gift is on the table the light shines
On it the sunlight brings out the colors
That the gift holds / Look at how brilliant
All the colors seems to be in this light

LAURA'S DILEMMA

A couple shag
Noisily

In a Fiat 500
On her road

On the Heath
Broom and

Forsythia bloom
Finches sing

It must be Spring

THE MOCKINGBIRD

Are you mocking me?
The bird asked,
Angrily.

SUNRISE

The silence
Of

The extinct
Ivory-

Billed
Wood-

Peck-
Er

Res-
Onates

Thru the
Park

Michael Gregory Stephens is the author of 29 books, including such poetry and prose poem collections as *Alcohol Poems, Paragraphs, Tangun Legend, Circles End, Translations* (from Korean), *Jigs and Reels, After Asia, Occam's Razor,* and *Top Boy.* More recently he published the hybrid work, *History of Theatre or the Glass of Fashion* (MadHat Press, 2021), as well as a novel about Modernist poet Ezra Pound entitled *King Ezra* (Spuyten Duyvil, 2022). In 2023, as well as *Ornithology,* Stephens will have a collection of stories, *Jesus' Dog,* published. Next year his memoir *When Poetry Was the World* is due out.

Printed in the USA
CPSIA information can be obtained
at www.ICGtesting.com
BVHW040700310723
667993BV00003B/206